**SEE TO
LEARN**

For Sydney, with love — KMG

For my husband, Michael — KP

Forest

Kate Moss Gamblin

Pictures by
Karen Patkau

GROUNDWOOD BOOKS
HOUSE OF ANANSI PRESS
TORONTO   BERKELEY

What do you see when you see a forest floor?

Do you see feet — yours and mine — and
the marks of others who have crossed this
path, on hoof or paw?

Do you see the animals that call this place home — the ants and worms, the spiders and all the very tiny creatures within the soil?

Do you see the shadow of the hawk as it soars above, hunting its next meal, or the swoop of the swallow in flight?

Do you see the pine needles, chestnut, oak and maple leaves all mixed together?

Do you see them gently falling all around,
making the soft carpet you now tread?

Do you see the great trees quietly standing,
facing all weathers, sharing their

presence — like their cousins in forests the world over?

Do you see the moss-covered stump of this ancient tree, old in the time of your grandparents' grandparents, returning to this Earth?

Do you see, alongside it, a caterpillar inching up a young sapling, both still becoming?

Do you see the clouds drifting above these sheltering branches, changing moment by moment, yet holding the promise of shade and rain?

Do you see the delicious sunlight, giving
way to the soft darkness of night?

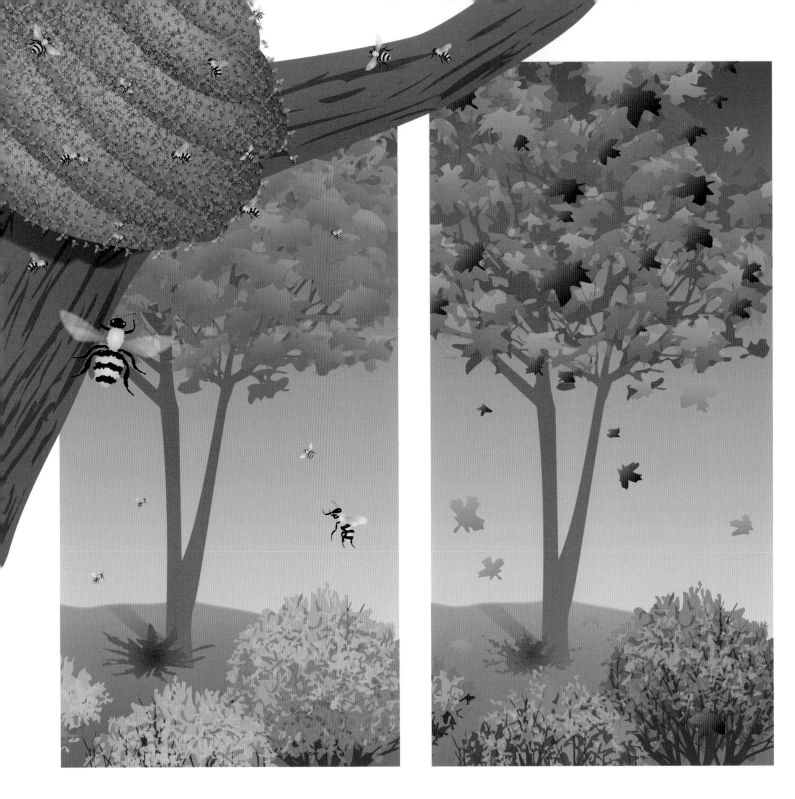

Do you see, over time, the ever-changing
seasons — the warm hum of summer's bees,
the fall of autumn's leaves,

the silence of winter's snows, the sprouting
life of spring?

Do you see the blush of the flowers' many petals among the thousands of shades of green, from darkest pine to brightest new leaf?

Do you see the invitation of the forest,
weaving all our lives together?
What do you see when you see a forest?

Author's Note

The See to Learn series supports young readers and their adult co-readers to engage with our delightful Earth in a fresh way. It is an everyday invitation to a living sense of wonder, to connect deeply not only to the natural world but also with ideas about it, to be awake to choices in caring for ourselves and our planet, to believe that our lives and choices make a difference, and to bring awareness to our thinking as a driver of our impact on the environment.

This series consciously moves beyond a straightforward appreciation of nature. It touches on aspects of a manner of perception available to each of us, our sustainability perspective, shaped by a sense of
- time in the present, extending into the past and future;
- place, both here and relating to other places near and far away;
- imagination for visioning what is not immediate;
- change which is ongoing at various speeds;
- relationship with each part and the whole, for both living and non-living;
- scale, covering the very tiniest to the very greatest and all in between;
- enough, within the bounds of a finite planet.

The series is grounded in research from my doctorate in sustainability learning and is imbued with love and gratitude for our precious, incomparable planetary home, along with hopefulness that we may shape a liveable future as we See to Learn.

Further Reading

For Young Readers:

Because of an Acorn by Lola M. Schaefer and Adam Schaefer, illustrated
    by Frann Preston-Gannon. Chronicle Books, 2016.
City Dog, Country Frog by Mo Willems, illustrated by Jon J. Muth.
    Disney-Hyperion, 2010.
Good Morning, Neighbor by Davide Cali, illustrated by Maria Dek.
    Princeton Architectural Press, 2018.
The Great Kapok Tree: A Tale of the Amazon Rain Forest by Lynne Cherry.
    HMH Books for Young Readers, 1990.
It Starts with a Seed by Laura Knowles, illustrated by Jennie Webber.
    words and pictures, 2017.
Rachel Carson and Her Book That Changed the World by Laurie Lawlor,
    illustrated by Laura Beingessner. Holiday House, 2012.
The Street Beneath My Feet by Charlotte Guillain, illustrated by Yuval
    Zommer. words and pictures, 2017.
Tokyo Digs a Garden by Jon-Erik Lappano, illustrated by Kellen
    Hatanaka. Groundwood Books, 2016.
Wangari's Trees of Peace: A True Story from Africa by Jeanette Winter.
    Harcourt Children's Books, 2008.
You Are Stardust by Elin Kelsey, illustrated by Soyeon Kim. Owlkids,
    2012.

For Older Readers:

The Lost Words by Robert Macfarlane, illustrated by Jackie Morris. House
    of Anansi Press, 2018.
The Sense of Wonder by Rachel Carson, photographs by Nick Kelsh.
    HarperCollins, 1998.

Text copyright © 2019 by Kate Moss Gamblin
Illustrations copyright © 2019 by Karen Patkau
Published in Canada and the USA in 2019 by Groundwood Books

Groundwood Books / House of Anansi Press
groundwoodbooks.com

We gratefully acknowledge for their financial support of our publishing program the Canada Council for the Arts, the Ontario Arts Council and the Government of Canada.

Canada Council   Conseil des Arts
for the Arts   du Canada

ONTARIO ARTS COUNCIL
CONSEIL DES ARTS DE L'ONTARIO
an Ontario government agency
un organisme du gouvernement de l'Ontario

With the participation of the Government of Canada
Avec la participation du gouvernement du Canada   Canada

Library and Archives Canada Cataloguing in Publication
Gamblin, Kate Moss, author
Forest / Kate Moss Gamblin ; illustrated by Karen Patkau.
(See to learn)
Issued in print and electronic formats.
ISBN 978-1-55498-879-2 (hardcover). — ISBN 978-1-55498-880-8 (PDF)
1. Forest ecology — Juvenile literature. 2. Forests and forestry — Juvenile literature. I. Patkau, Karen, illustrator II. Title.
QH541.5.F6G36 2019   j577.3   C2018-903739-3
C2018-903740-7

The artwork in *See to Learn: Forest* was digitally rendered.
Design by Michael Solomon
Printed and bound in Malaysia